PEACE, PATIENCE, & PETTY

A LITTLE BOOK OF COLORING, COPING, AND CUTTING FOLKS OFF (RESPECTFULLY)

a WellLit Studio production

by Regina M. Townsend

For resources, updates, or to connect across all of my projects, visit:
ReginaTownsend.com — the hub for Well Lit, The Broken Brown Egg, and more.

Hey Sis...

I'm glad you're here.

Wherever "here" is for you.

However you're arriving at this space, you belong.

Peace, **Patience** and **Petty** is designed for all the ones trying to navigate life without crashing out. And as the founder of one of the leading infertility organizations for people of color, I know that crash is super close when you're navigating reproductive health choices plus daily life.

I want this activity book to serve as a gentle reminder that growth is not linear, and healing is not one-size-fits-all.

Inside, you'll find coloring pages, reflection prompts, and affirmations designed to nurture your heart and honor your story.

There's no "right" way to feel—just your way.

With love and solidarity,

Your Homegirl, Regina

Color Test Page

Give your markers or colored pencils a try before you start coloring.

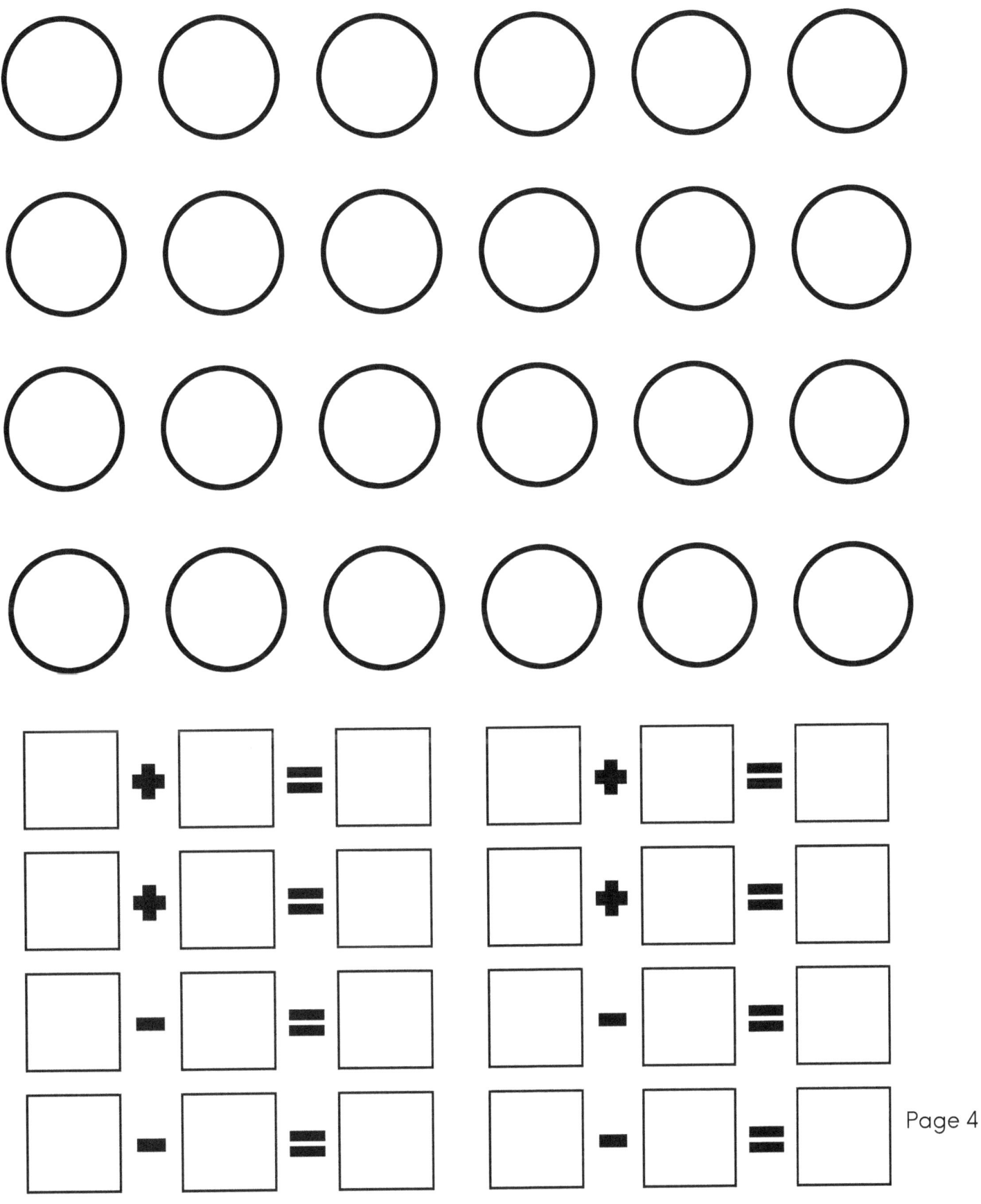

SOME OF THIS JOURNEY GRANTS

PEACE.

SOME OF THIS JOURNEY TEACHES

PATIENCE,

& SOME OF THIS JOURNEY REQUIRES

PETTY

The Feelings Jar

Because sometimes "fine" just won't cut it.
Give each feeling a color (blue = calm, yellow = joy, red = annoyed).
When you check in, pick the color that matches your mood for real.
Fill in a star.
Watch your jar fill up with proof that you're allowed to feel every last one of your emotions — even the messy ones.

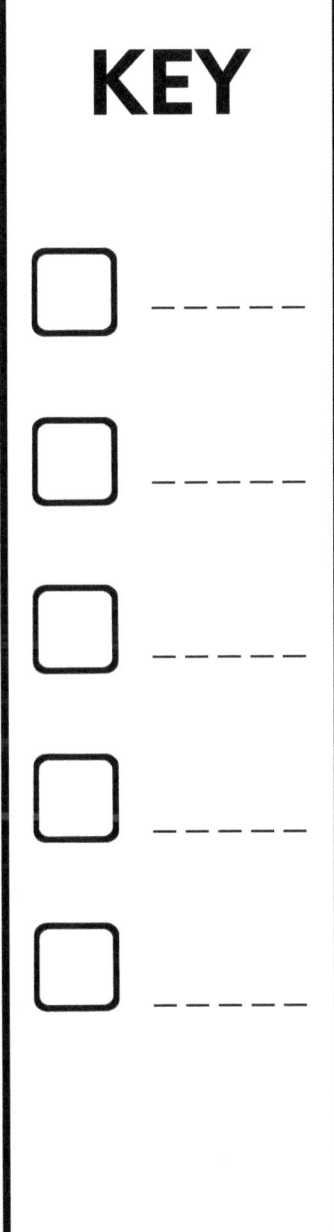

FILLING MY JAR

KEY

LETTER TO MYSELF

Write a letter to your body,...even the parts you're pissed at.

Today I Might...

- ☐ Sit under a blanket
- ☐ Say no to that text
- ☐ Drink water slowly
- ☐ Do absolutely nothing and call it rest

CUSS EM OUT, SIS

Mama nem, cousin nem, nosy coworker, or even frenemy. Let them have it.

_____

_____

_____

_____

_____

_____

_____

_____

_____

_____

_____

_____

_____

MY HOMEGIRL
REGINA
SAID FOR YOU TO
MIND YOUR
BUSINESS

_____

_____

_____

_____

_____

_____

_____

_____

_____

_____

ving the PCOS life...

retty
onfident
ptimistic
uccessful

ROOTED & Rising

A Blooming Meditation

Find a comfortable sea
Let your hands rest gen
in your lap or at your side
Close your eyes, if you fe
safe doing so.
Inhale slowly through yo
nose... and exhale softly
With each breath, imag
yourself as a seed, plant
in rich soil.

Supported. Safe.
Breathe in: possibility.
Breathe out: pressure.

Picture roots extending
from you into the earth-
anchoring you in streng
wisdom, and love.

Now picture a tender
green sprout reaching
upward.
That's you—still rising.

Repeat quietly to yourse
"I am rooted. I am rising
am enough."

Take one more deep
breath in... and out.

When you're ready, gen
wiggle your fingers, and
return to the room.

She Believed She Could,... But Then Her Uterus Said No.

My cracks don't break me, they crown me.

Kintsugi is the Japanese art of repairing broken pottery with gold.

It reminds us that cracks aren't flaws — they're part of our beauty.

Translation: what tried to break you just made you more valuable.

Stay crowned.

Journaling Prompts

- I wish I'd known to...

- I wish I could say...

- I wish someone would tell me...

- A moment I've felt seen was...

- I love myself because...

- I give myself permission to...

- My story matters because...

- What is something you've survived that you didn't think you could?

  - What does rest look like for you today?

  - What would you say if you could just let it all out?

  - Write a letter to yourself 5 years from now.

  - Make a list of what you need right now.

    - The part of me that's exhausted wants to say...

    - Right now I need..

      - What's one small thing you can do today to take care of yourself, even if it's just for five minutes?

SHIT I NEED TO SAY

Whatever that may be.

_____

_____

_____

_____

_____

_____

_____

_____

_____

_____

_____

_____

_____

_____

_____

_____

_____

_____

_____

_____

_____

THINGS I'M NO LONGER EXPLAINING

Some answers will be horizontal, some vertical, and some will only make sense if you've been through a season of choosing yourself.

```
E X S O E T U E C L B L O C K E D Z H
R L X X I W K N W G C O T J E J I I I Q
G Y Q G S G B S S T R E J L H F V P T E
R S I L E N C E J H U O B X W G W R T F
L R S S B G B B M S R A W P Z J G I D R
S A Y I N G N O V U L B U T J G P O O L
V C H W M X V B D I Y N W M H M U R D T
M X L Z X D E L A Y E D R E P L Y I B R
Z V K Z X H W V P D B I D Z W U P T P E
Q G Y U Y W A W P G O F O E M N C I E S
S L L X S N R D S O F T L I F E X E A T
N T H Q U Z O K C O I M Y F A C E S C W
E M O T I O N A L L A B O R D E Z Z E V
O G T H M G H O S T I N G B U Q T Z O S
P R O T E C T I N G M Y P E A C E I A O
B O U N D A R I E S H E A L I N G L U K
E N E R G Y V N O T T O D A Y Y U W O J
T I R E D Z U N O T G O I N G L D U L Q
C S K V R E C H A R G I N G H S I O K D
Q K S A I L Q K M T H E R A P Y E X C L
```

Boundaries	Unavailable	Healing
Mood	Soft Life	Not Today
Silence	Blocked	Growth
Saying No	Recharging	
Rest	Emotional Labor	
Not Going	Priorities	
Energy	Therapy	
Ghosting	Tired	
Peace	My Face	
Delayed Reply	Protecting My Peace	

Sorry,
CAN'T HEAR YOU OVER MY HOPE.

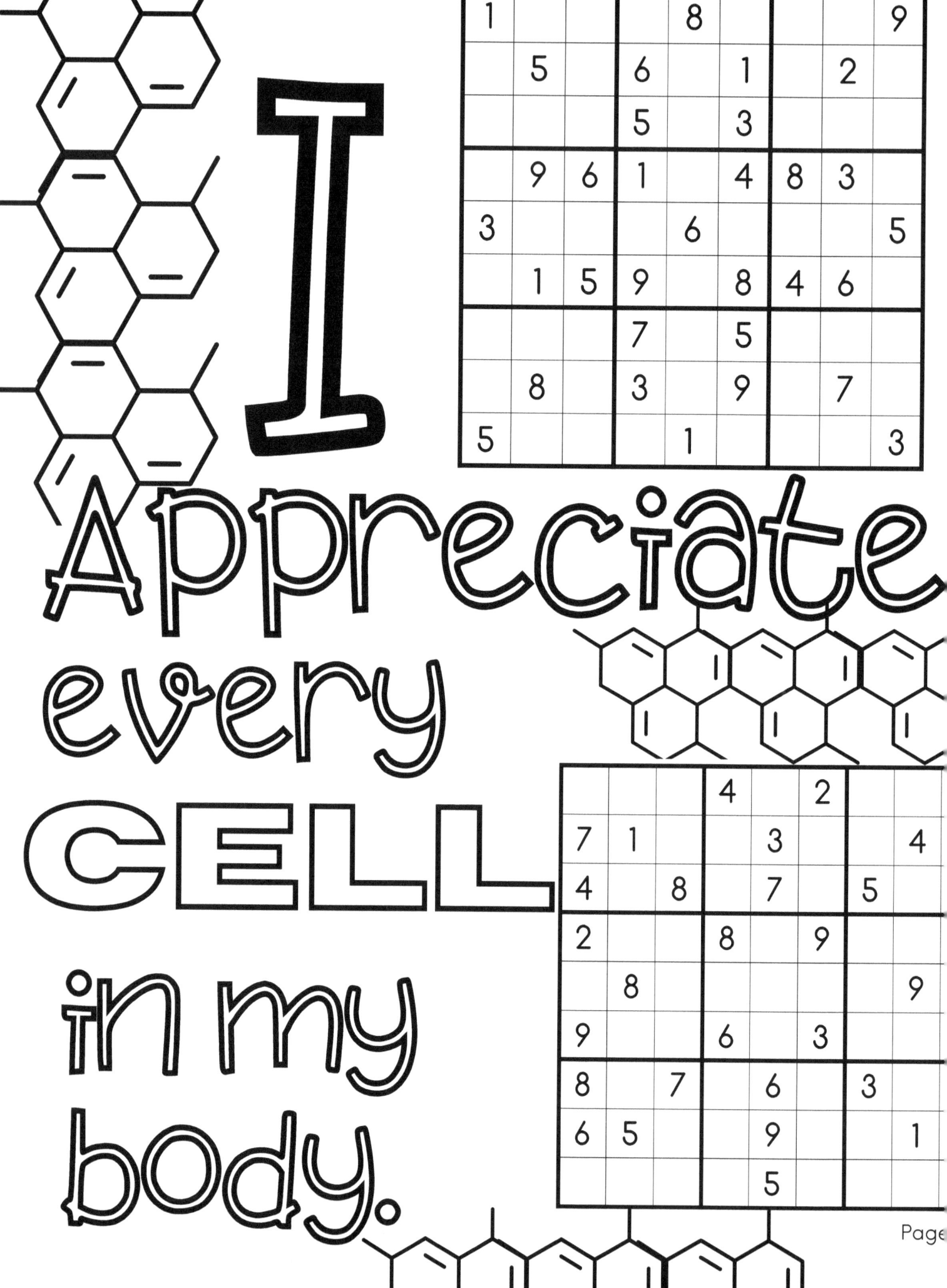

BUILD YOUR OWN OTTERLY AMAZING COMMUNITY

Otters hold hands when they sleep
so they don't drift apart.
They float in rafts, rest on their backs,
and let go of what's too heavy.
You can too.
Let it drift.
Find your raft.
Rest easy.

Sometimes it feels like every choice has an invoice... but trust yourself.

INFERTILITY IS BIGGER THAN BABIES

READY TO BREAK THROUGH

MY Body is healing AND I FEEL BETTER Every day

Bloom Affirmations

My story is still unfolding.

I am blooming at my own pace.

I deserve tenderness, even on hard days.

I honor my healing, no matter what it looks like.

I carry strength in my softness.

This season is still sacred.

LETTER TO "THAT" DOCTOR

To the one who didn't hear you, couldn't see you, or flat out ignored you...

_____
_____
_____
_____
_____
_____
_____
_____
_____
_____
_____
_____
_____

_____
_____
_____
_____
_____
_____
_____
_____
_____
_____
_____
_____

Hold Up, Doc,...

repeat that again for my voice memo.

REMEMBER,

today may be the day I saved
bail money for....

so talk to me nice!

BEFORE YOU GO...

For more wit, wisdom, and words from Regina, check out;

Make IF Make Sense: Putting Words to the Feels of Infertility
Part memoir, part journal, all heart — this book helps you unpack the emotional rollercoaster of infertility with honesty, humor, and hope.
Available now in ebook & paperback

Follow @brokenbrownegg on Instagram
and tag your colored pages with #PeacePatiencePetty

Need more resources?
www.reginatownsend.com

If this work helped you feel seen, please share it with someone who needs it.